The Legend of the 14 Underwater Creatures

WRITTEN BY ALICE WANG
ILLUSTRATED BY PETER WONG

CONTENTS

Introduction

"In the beginning God created the heavens and the earth.

And God said, 'Let the water under the sky be gathered to one place, and let dry ground appear.' And it was so. God called the dry ground 'land,' and the gathered waters He called 'seas.' And God saw that it was good.

And God said, 'Let the water teem with living creatures, and let birds fly above the earth across the vault of the sky.' So God created the great creatures of the sea and every living thing with which the water teems and that moves about in it, according to their kinds..." (Genesis 1: 1, 9-10, 20-21)

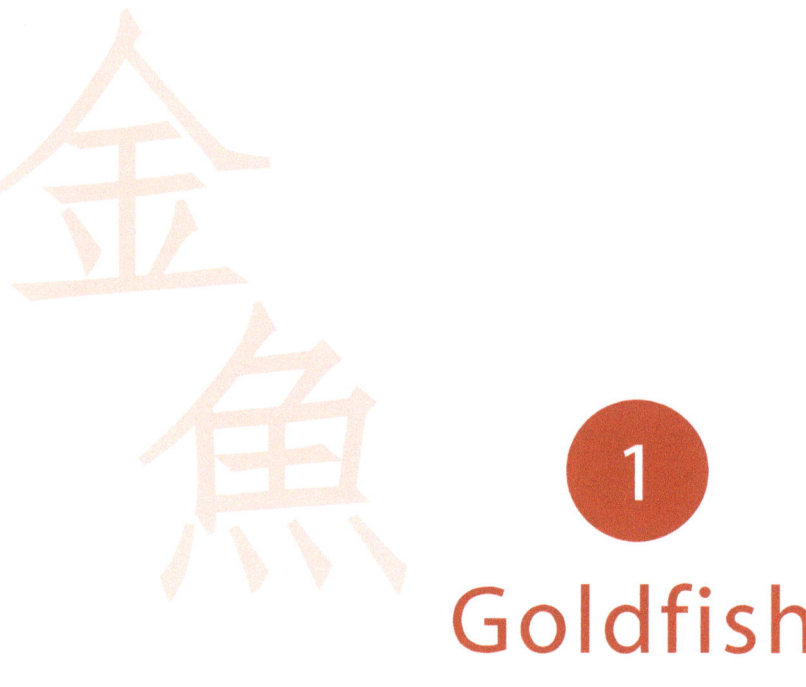

1

Goldfish

In the rivers of Asia, the beautiful Oranda Goldfish swims. It looks up and sees God's loving face, bright as the sun. The goldfish does a little dance, its orange scales shining in the light, its long tails twirling like a silk dress. The empress of ancient China in the Song Dynasty made a grand pond just for the gold and red Oranda Goldfish, and people around the world believed these goldfishes could bring them wealth and good things.

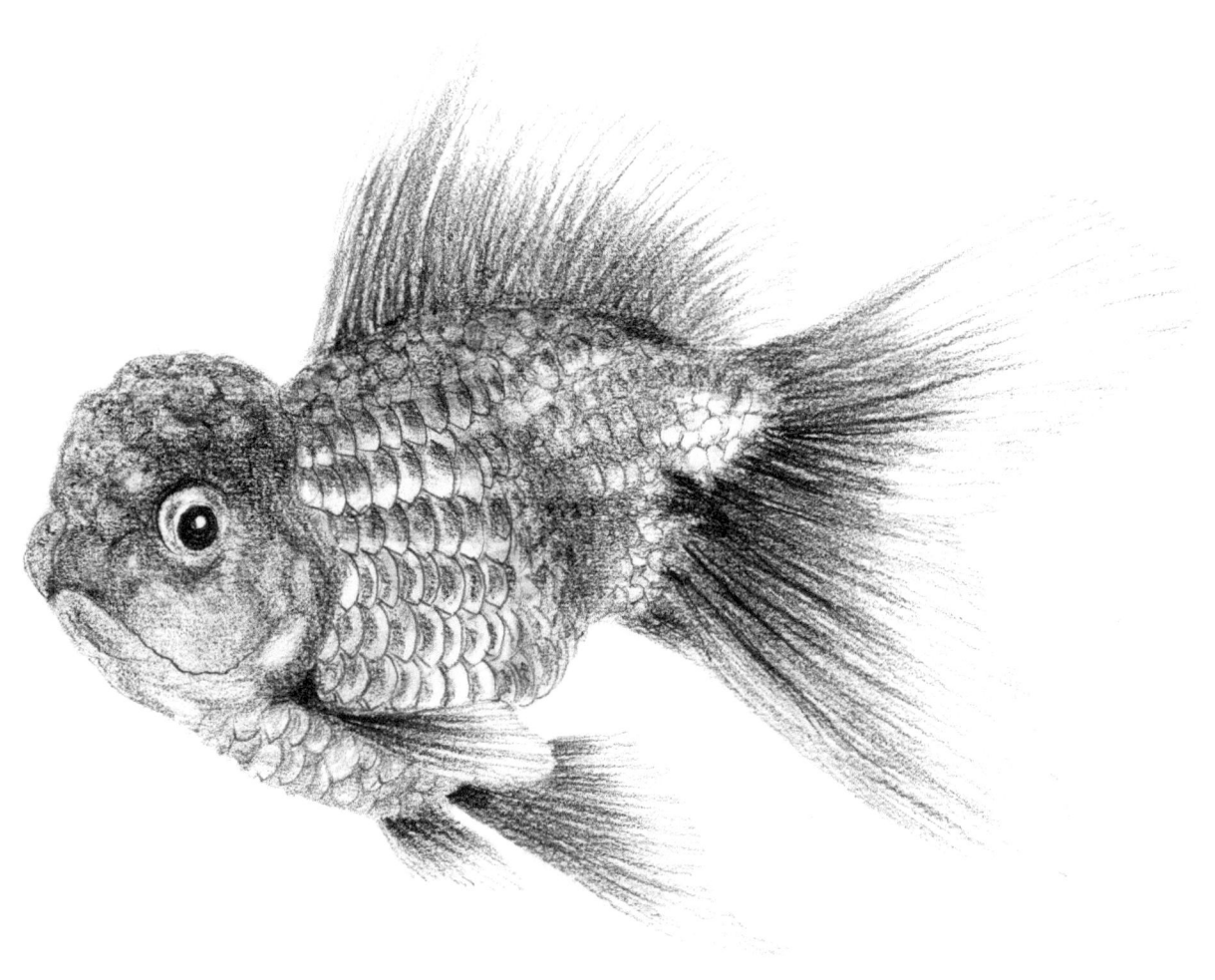

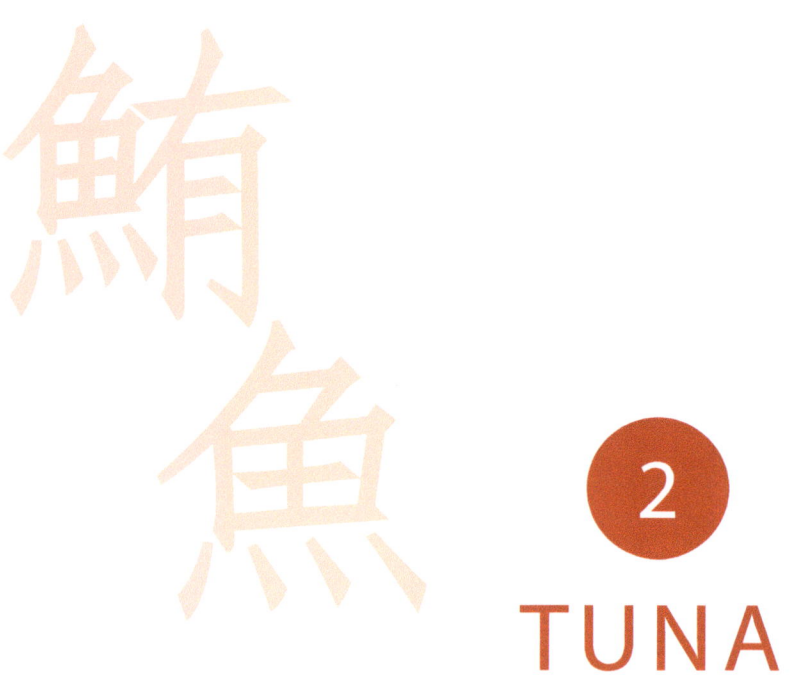

2

TUNA

In the temperate North Pacific Ocean, off the East Asia coast, lived the Pacific Bluefin Tuna. God made the tuna warm-blooded, different from the other fishes that are mostly cold-blooded. Because of this gift, the tuna is an extra fast swimmer, able to swim more than 30 miles per hour! The tuna suddenly swims away fast as a rocket because right behind it is a hungry…

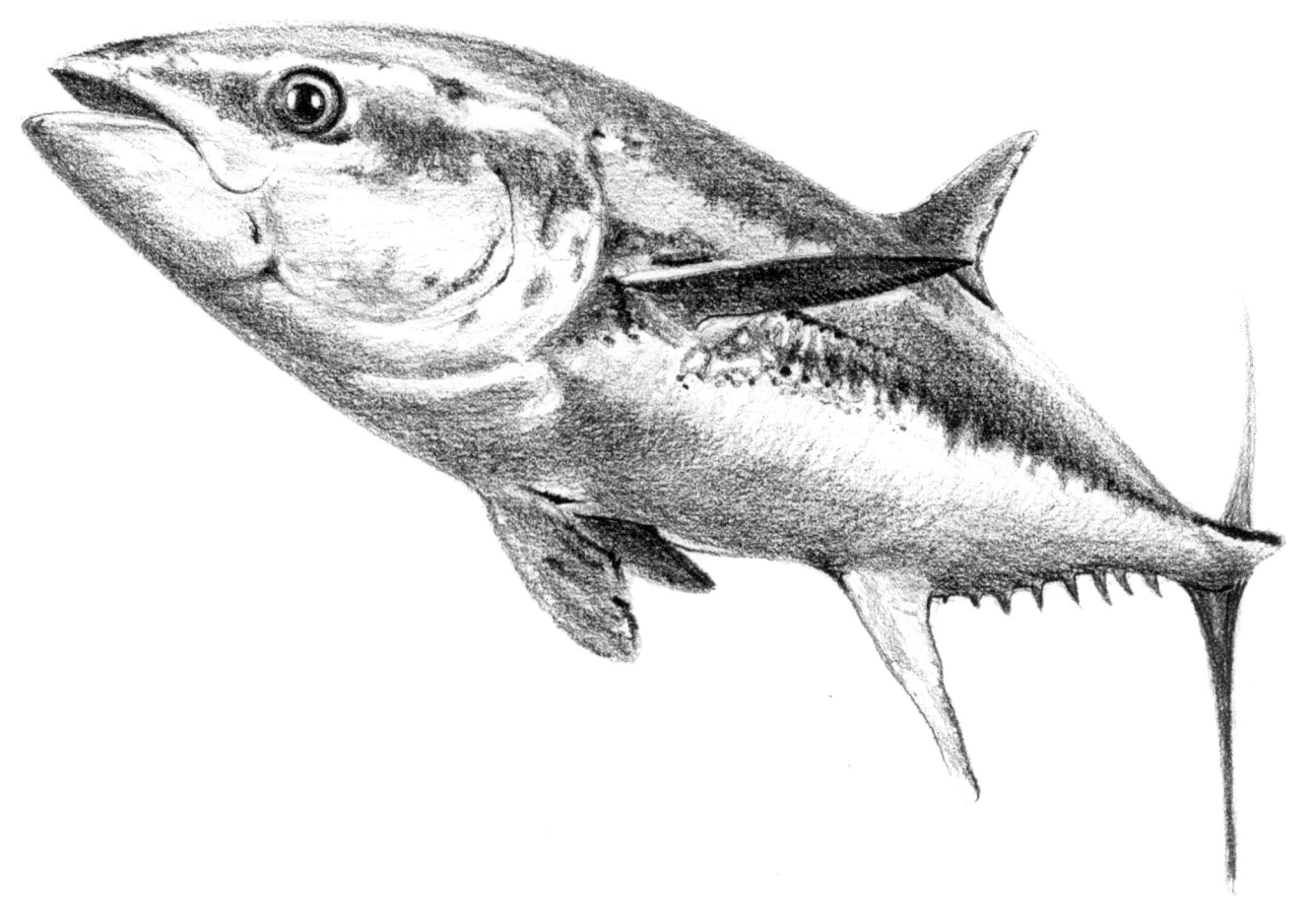

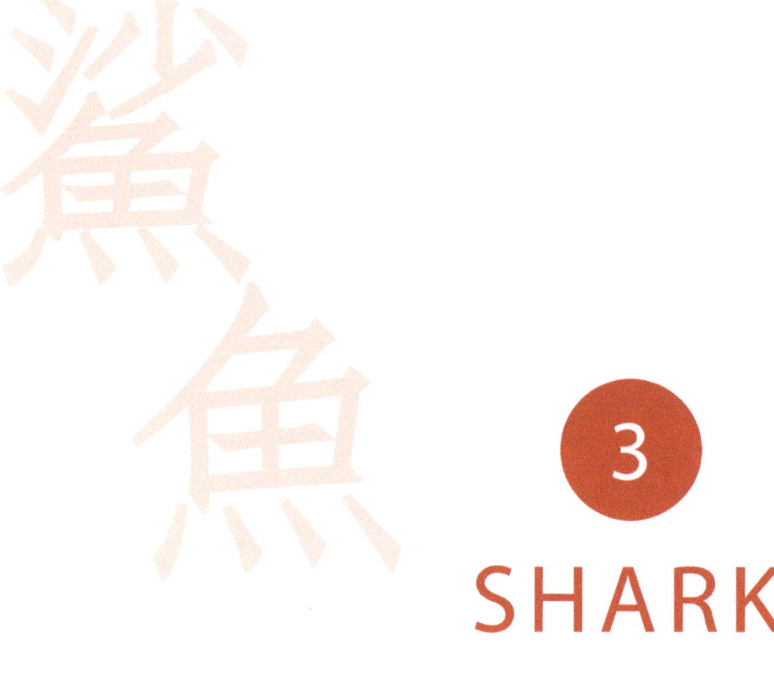

3
SHARK

…Great White Shark! Its mouth is wide open, showing rows and rows of
razor-sharp teeth. The shark missed its meal, but not to worry,
God had given the shark a special ability – a sixth sense
that allows the shark to find other hiding prey.
The shark can detect the electromagnet fields that all living things produce,
so even fish hiding under the sand cannot escape the hunting shark.
Now off goes the shark to look for its dinner.

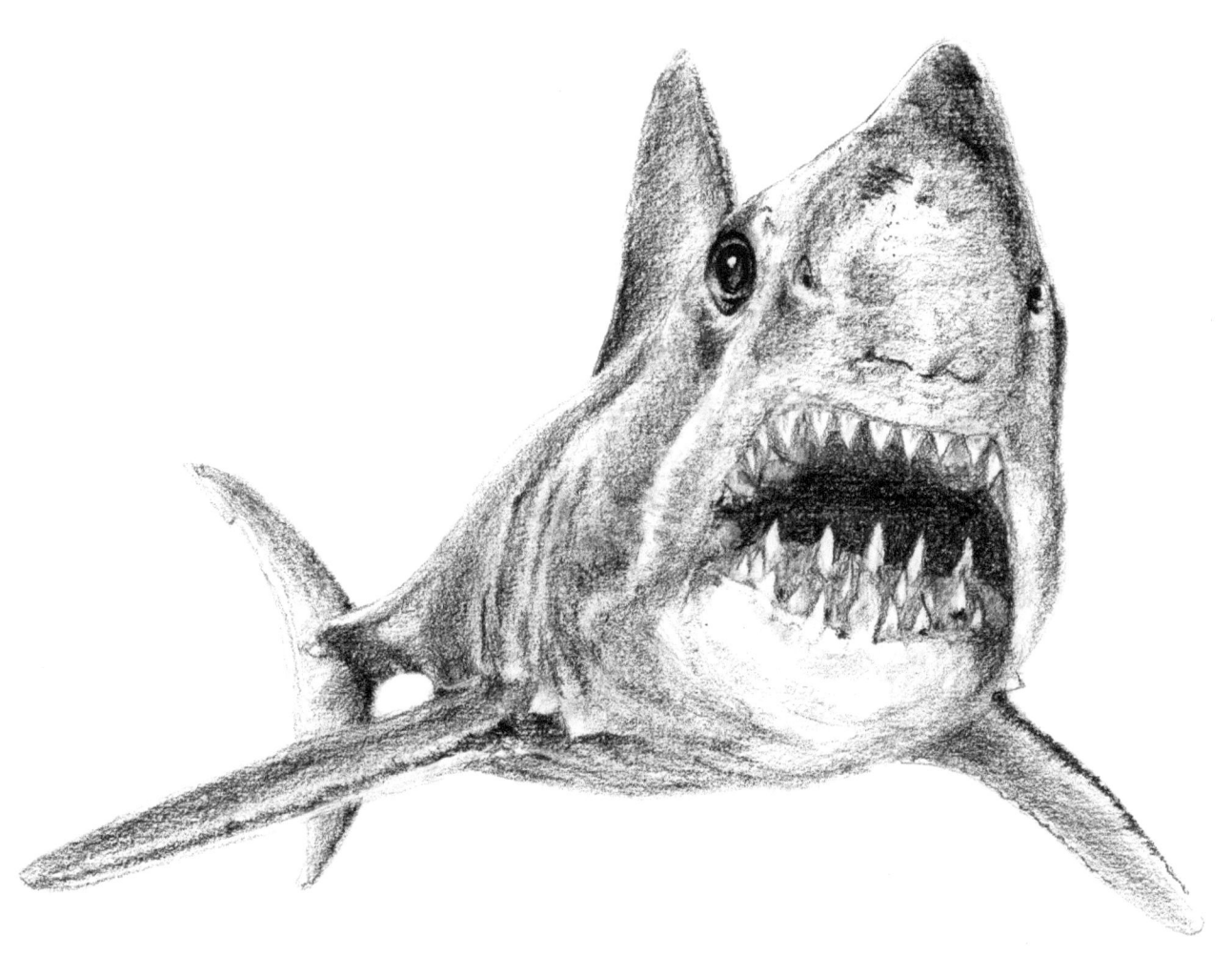

4 Sea Turtle

海龜

It is now nighttime, a Sea Turtle hauls herself onto the beach and begins
digging a large nest in the damp sand. She then fills the nest with her eggs,
covers the nest with sand, and returns to the ocean.
Two months later, the baby sea turtles hatch from the eggs,
struggle out of the nest, and race to the seawaters.
When sea turtles go under water to look for food or to sleep,
they can hold their breath for up to seven hours.
God blessed the ocean with these graceful creatures who protect
the sea grass beds that are important for the survival of many marine animals.

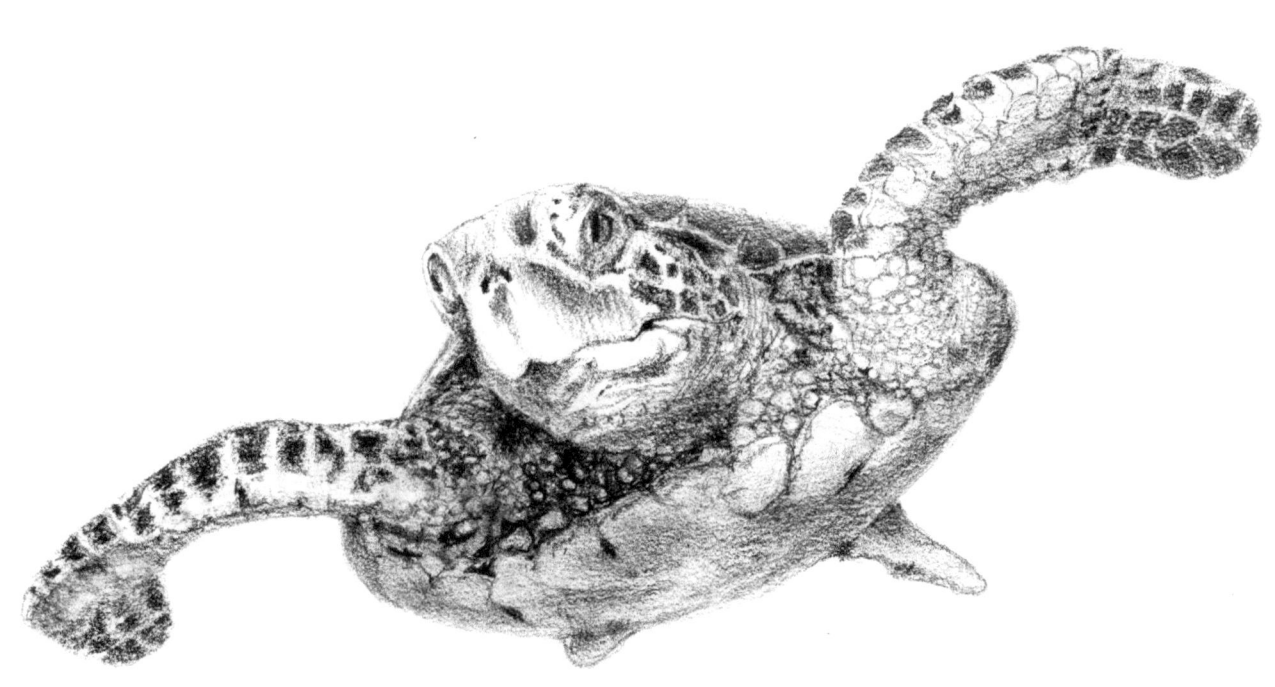

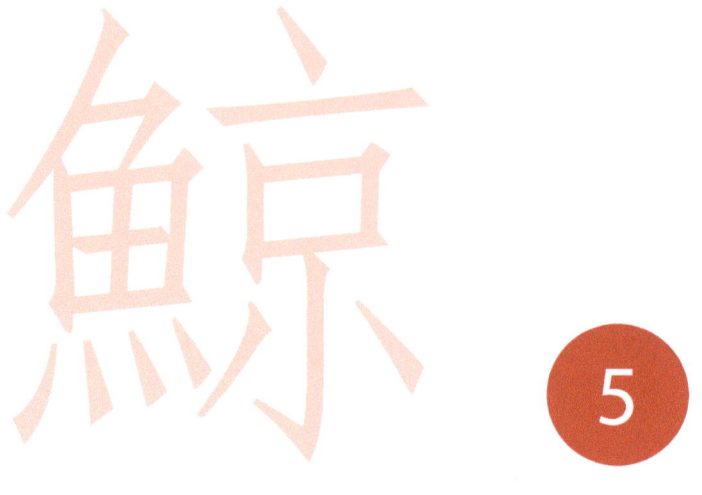

5

Humpback Whale

Do you hear that beautiful, echoing song in the deep seas?
It is the song of the Humpback Whale, a majestic creation of God
who has been documented to protect seals and other whales from Killer Whales.
The courageous Humpback Whale also reveals God's kindness in its
friendly interactions with other whale species.
The whale cares for its baby in the warm tropical seas
until the baby grows stronger after one to two years.

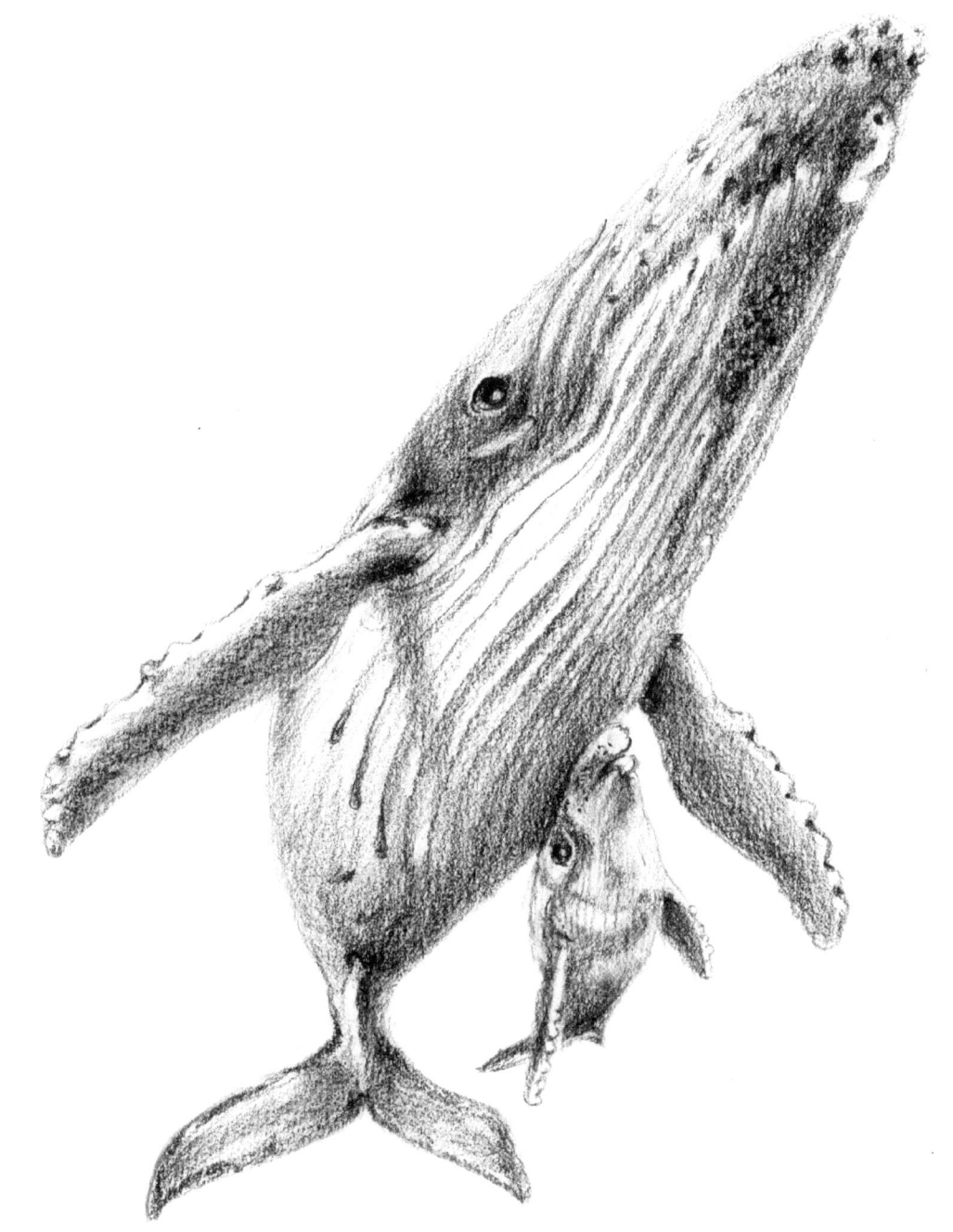

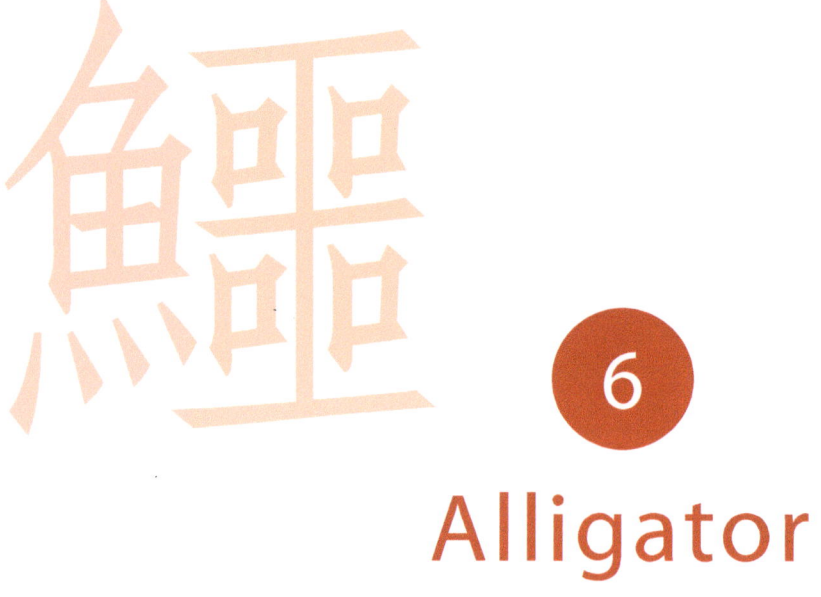

6

Alligator

Let us go now to the longest river in Asia, the Yangtze River of China,
and here we see the Alligator sprawling on its belly and slithering into the river.
God's strength is seen in the Alligator's powerful jaws,
which can tear apart large animals such as panthers and even bears.

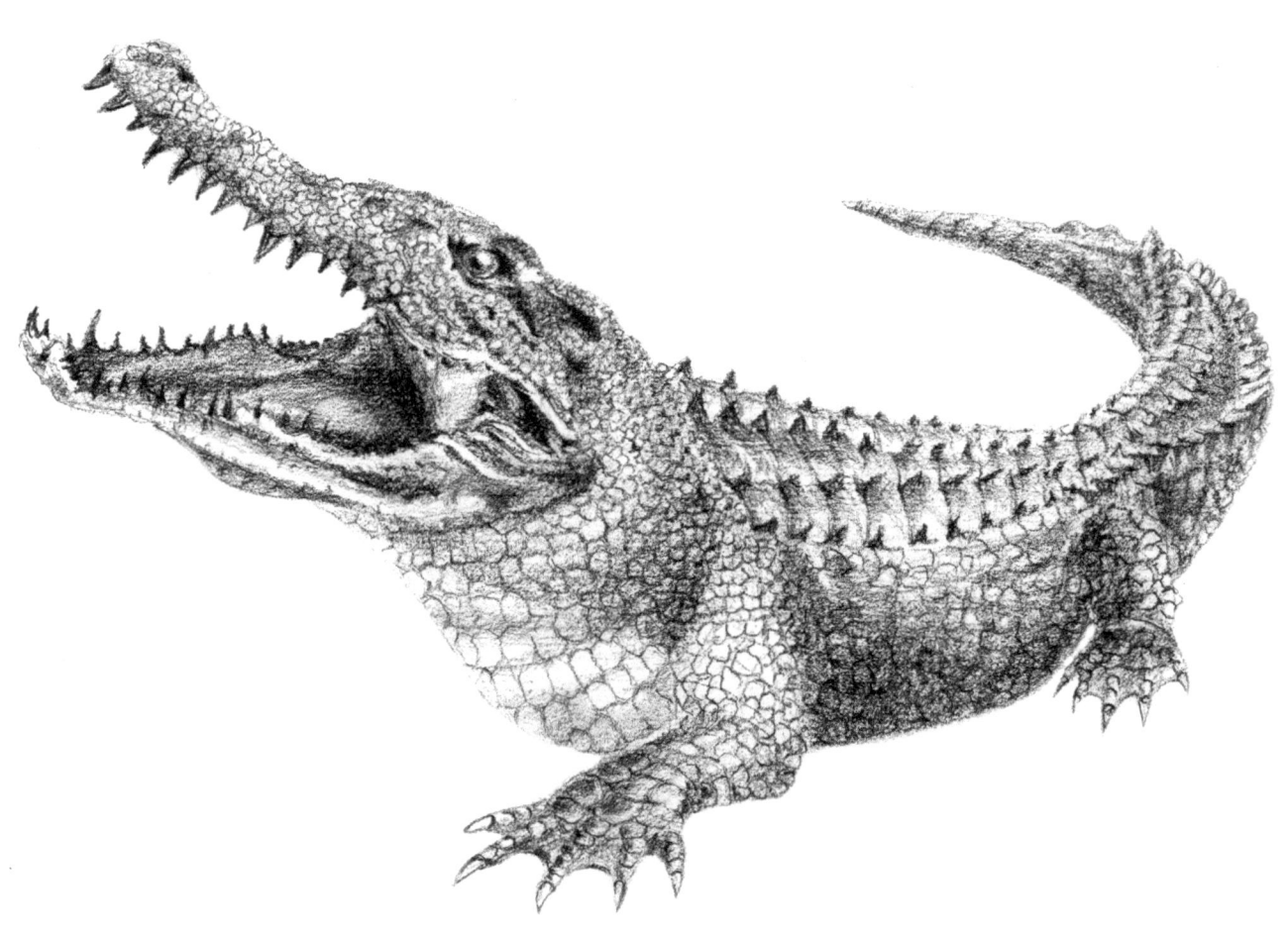

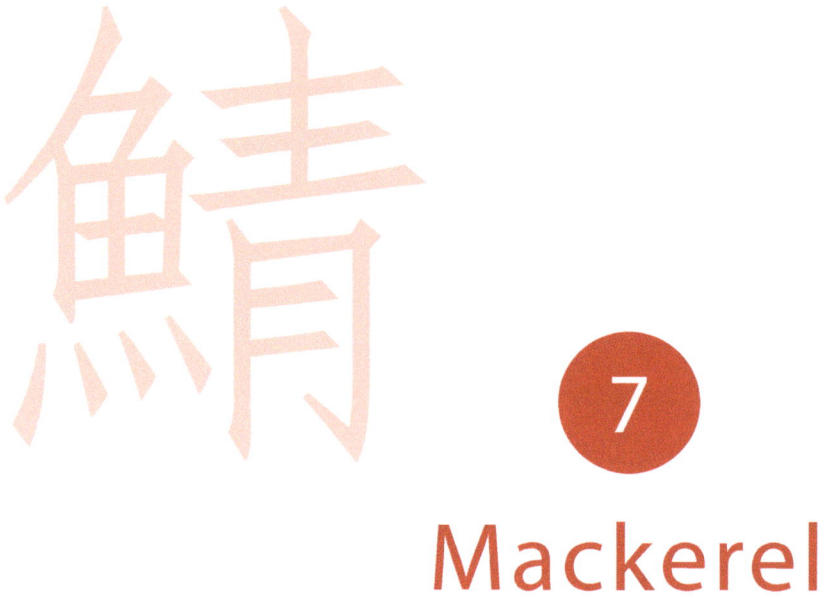

⑦ Mackerel

In the coasts of Brazil, we find the King Mackerel, a superb swimmer
that can retract its fins in for streamlining as it shoots across the Atlantic seas.
The King Mackerel cruises on long migrations at 10 kilometers per hour
moving to warmer waters in winter times and returning as the seasons change.
God taught the mackerels to travel in schools to protect each other
on their long journeys. The light-reflecting stripes on their backs
can signal one another to react quickly when feeding or escaping danger.

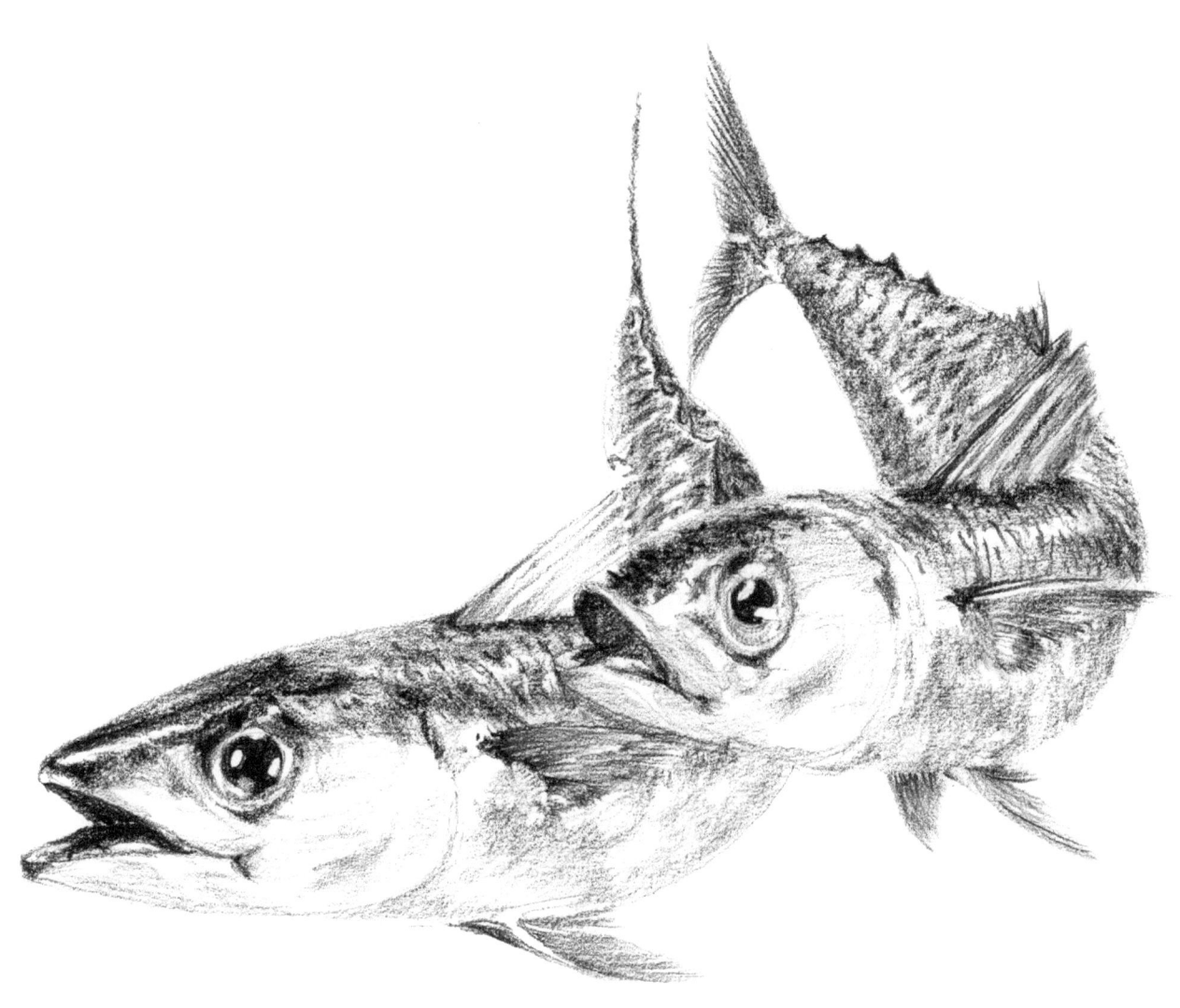

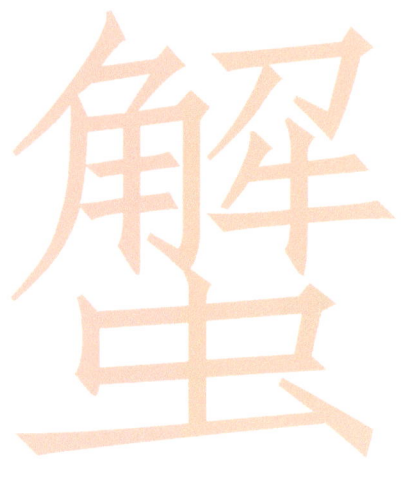

Crab

After the school of mackerels whooshed past in a silver swarm, we emerge at
the rocky seashores, where an eager Crab waves his giant claw
at a female crab in hopes of attracting her.
He dances about, hopping in and out of his burrow and drumming
with his claws – all to show her how strong and dependable he is.
God also gave crabs the gift of teamwork,
as crabs are known to work together to feed and protect their families.

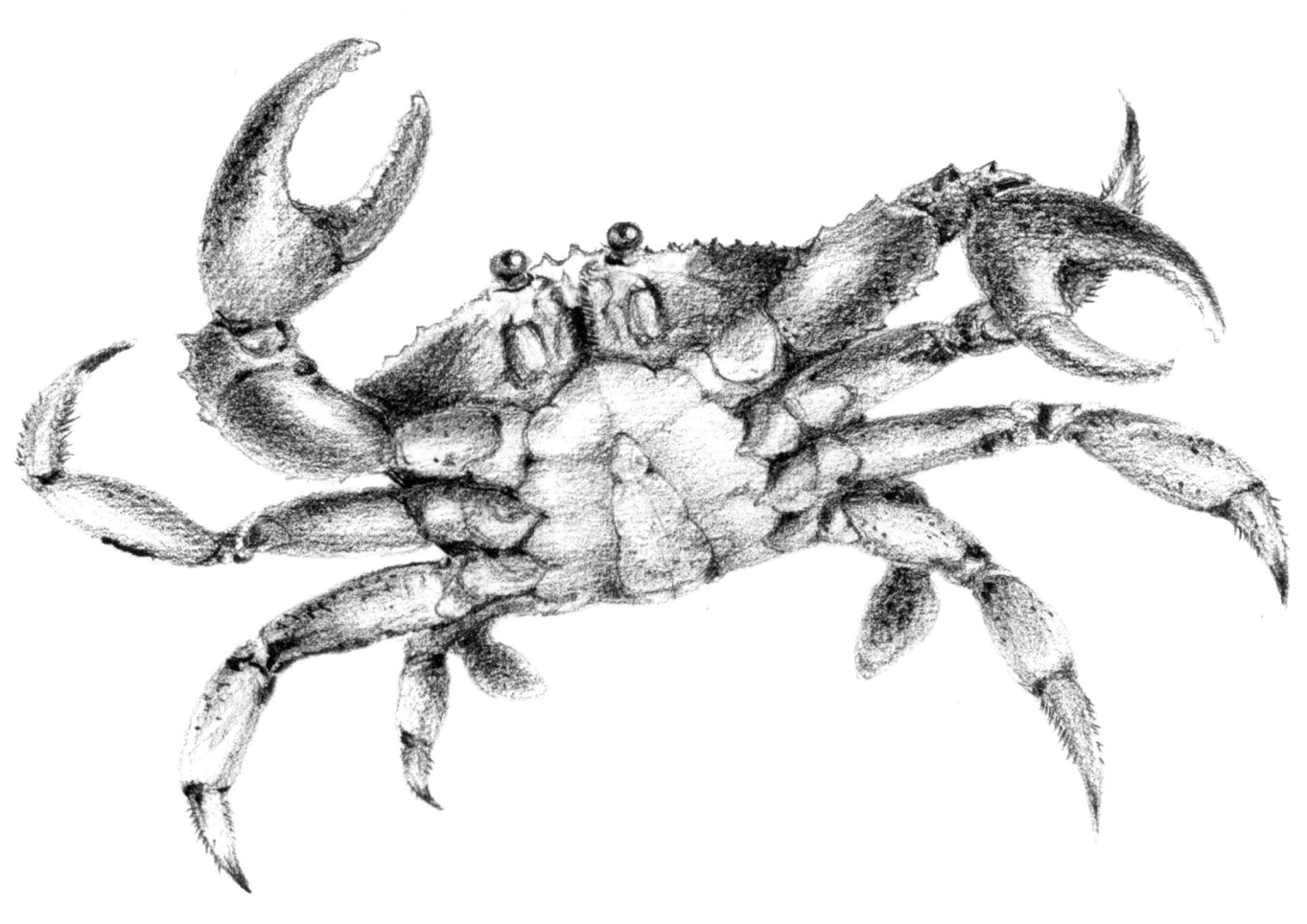

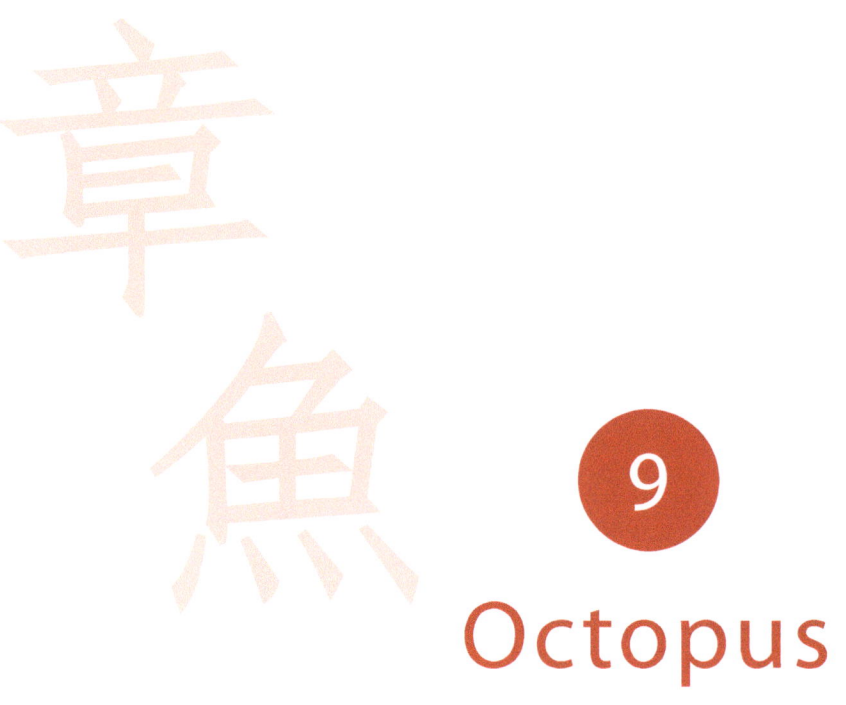

9

Octopus

Here among the coral reefs, we spot a giant creature slowly crawling about with its large head and eight squiggling tentacles. The Octopus is unlike any other sea creature with its great intelligence, sharp eyesight, and arms that move on their own. Octopuses have been shown to be able to solve mazes, store short and long-term memories, strategize, and learn. These creatures have even been known to climb aboard fishing ships and open containers of fish to eat.

God also gave the octopus skin that can transform to match its surroundings in color and even shape, making the octopus the great magician of the seas.

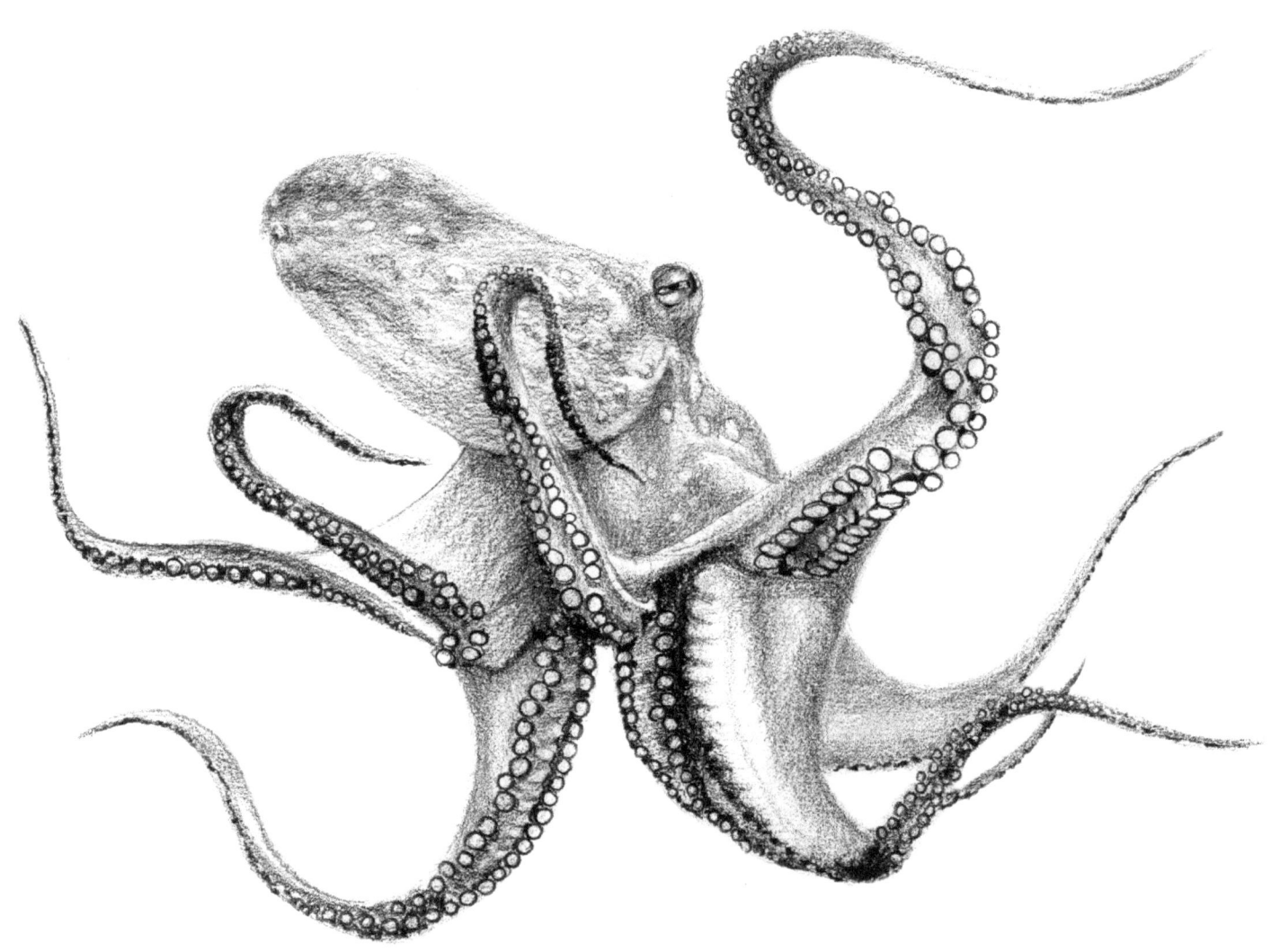

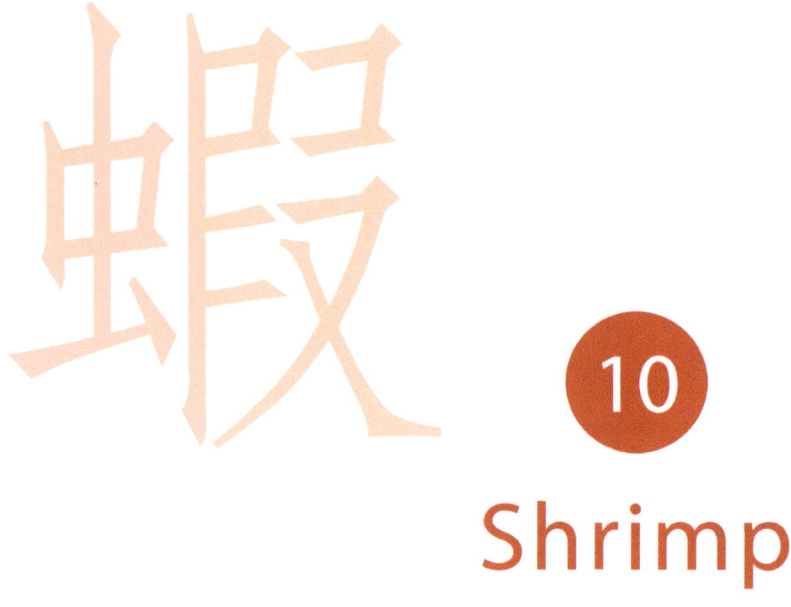

10

Shrimp

Do you hear the racket of what sounds like hundreds of pistols going off? That is the cacophony of the Pistol Shrimps, so loud in the ocean that submarines are unable to communicate when passing through these shrimp colonies; battle submarines even used such noise to hide from enemy detection. Though small in size, the shrimp is another important protector God gave to the ocean; some shrimp clean parasites from fish, others keep sea cucumbers healthy, and all are integral to life undersea.

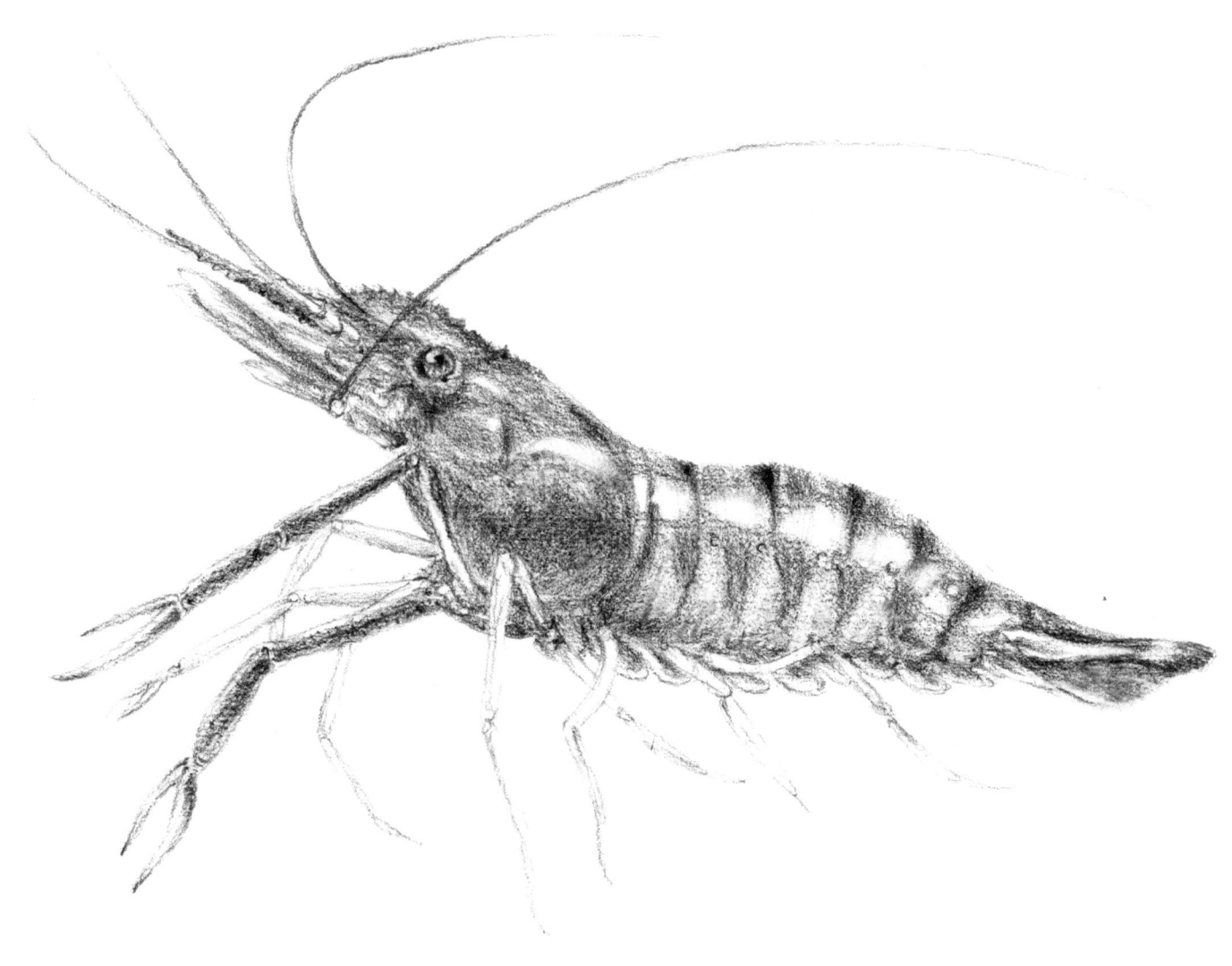

海豚

Dolphin

Do you see those bubbles rising up at the surface of the sea? Look down and you will see the snout and delightful grin of the Dolphin playfully creating bubble rings and breaking them up into smaller bubbles.

Besides a strong curiosity and capacity to learn and teach, God also gave dolphins the gift of unique identity: each Bottlenose Dolphin has a signature whistle and they can memorize each other's whistles to identify and communicate with one another. Dolphins are highly intelligent and some even partner with fishermen to help them catch fish.

These playful creatures demonstrate the goodness, beauty, and joy of God.

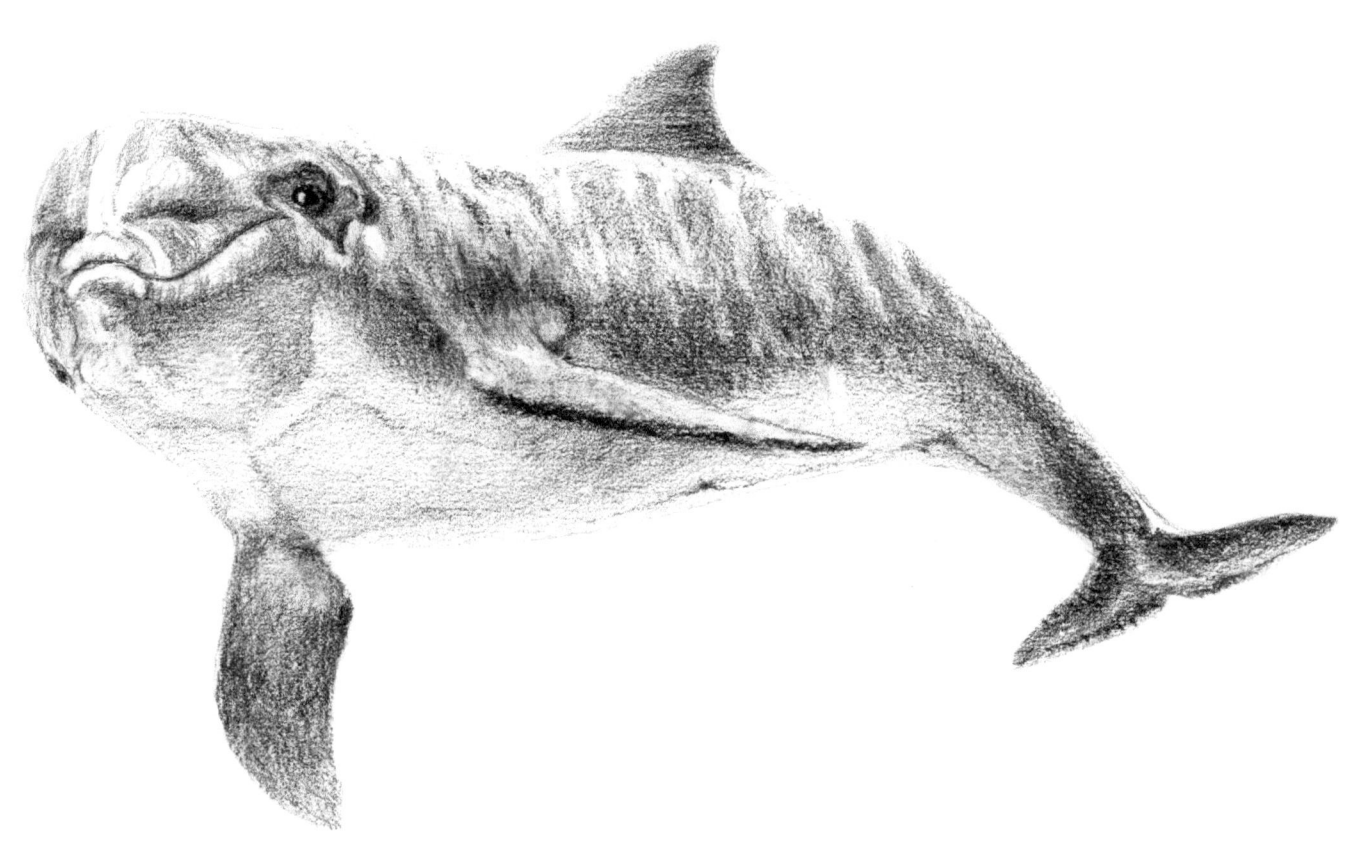

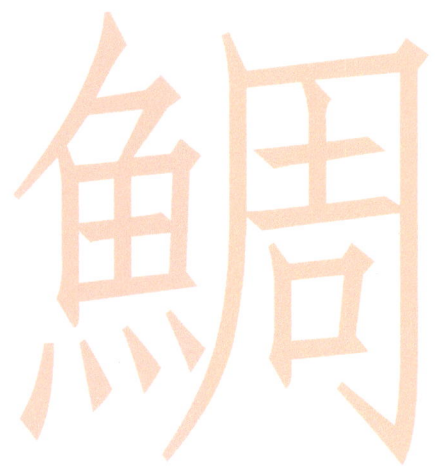

Pagrus Major

On the rough grounds of the South China Sea, we find the reddish Pagrus Majors.
The people of Japan, Korea, and Taiwan thank God for providing them with
the abundant supply of these fishes, which are seen as a blessing from heaven.
The Han Dynasty emperor of China once saw a red and golden colored
Pagrus Major jumped onto his ship. Since it was the emperor's birthday,
the fish was named jiageeyu – the fish that added blessings.

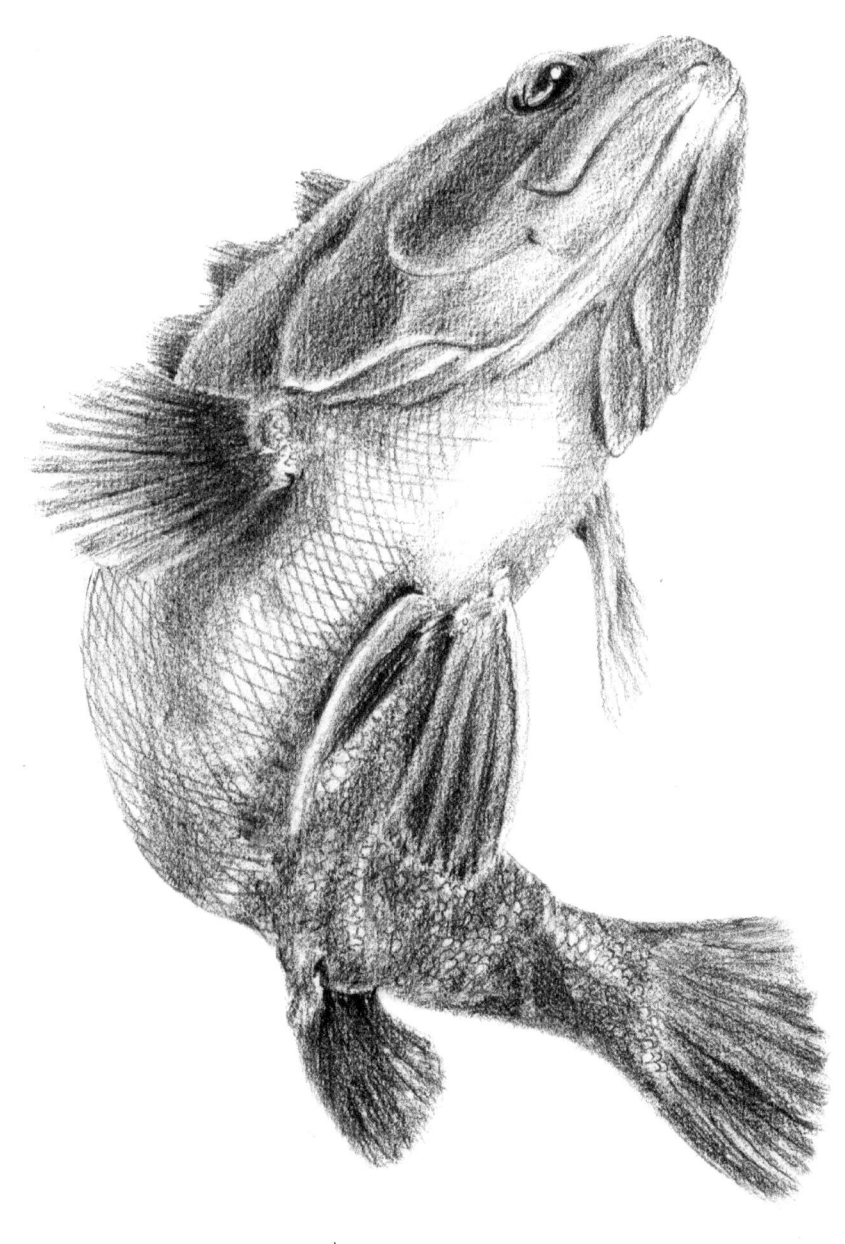

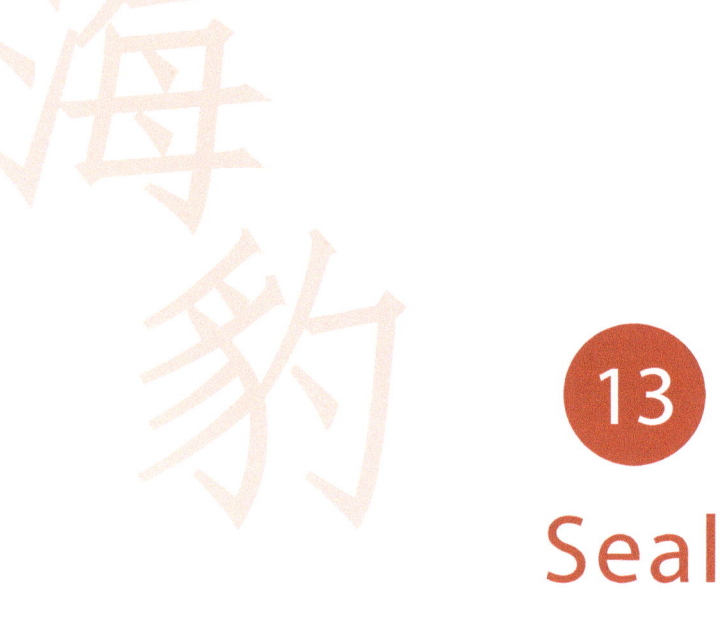

13

Seal

Let us now go to the top of the world – the North Pole. In a snow-white world covered with ice, we meet the baby Harper Seal. The furry baby seal is waiting for his mother, who has gone out to sea looking for food.
Mother seals fast to nurse their young and between feeding go on foraging trips that can last from a day to two weeks. But baby seal is not alone; he lives with a large and noisy colony of other harper seals.
God gave the seals special eyes with mobile pupils that adapt to the bright glare of the Arctic ice. The seals also have an amazing sense of smell that allows them to find their young and to sense predators.

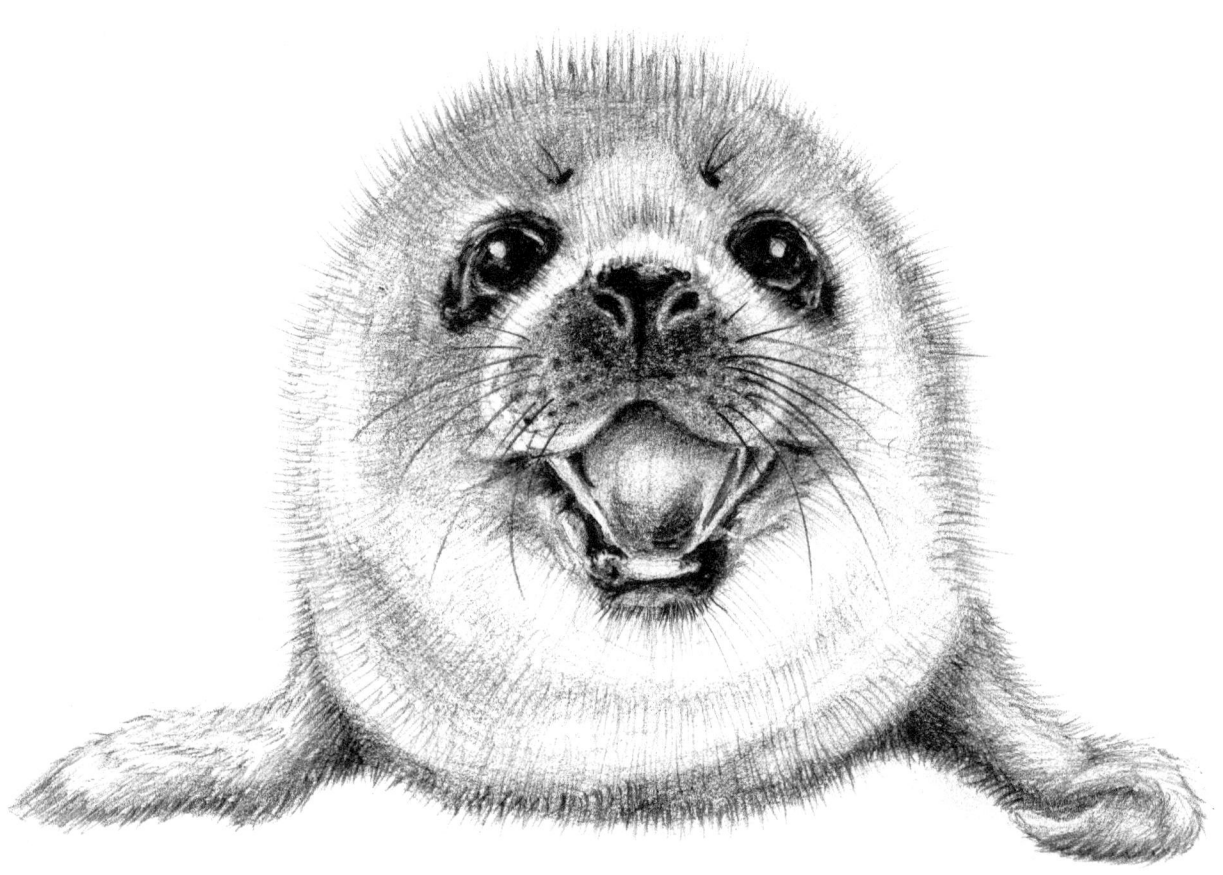

海獺

14

Sea Otter

In the North Pacific Ocean, we find a family of Sea Otters holding paws as they take an afternoon nap. To prevent themselves from drifting away, otters wrap themselves with kelp while sleeping. God blessed the ocean with otters to protect marine life by eating sea urchins, which chews and damages kelp forests. Otters are one of the few mammals that use tools – they can open hard shells and pry abalone off with rocks. Otters are also very playful in the way they make waterslides and play with stones. As we end our adventure with the aquatic creatures, we join the sea otter to say a peaceful and thankful prayer to our God, who has created this wondrous and diverse underwater world.

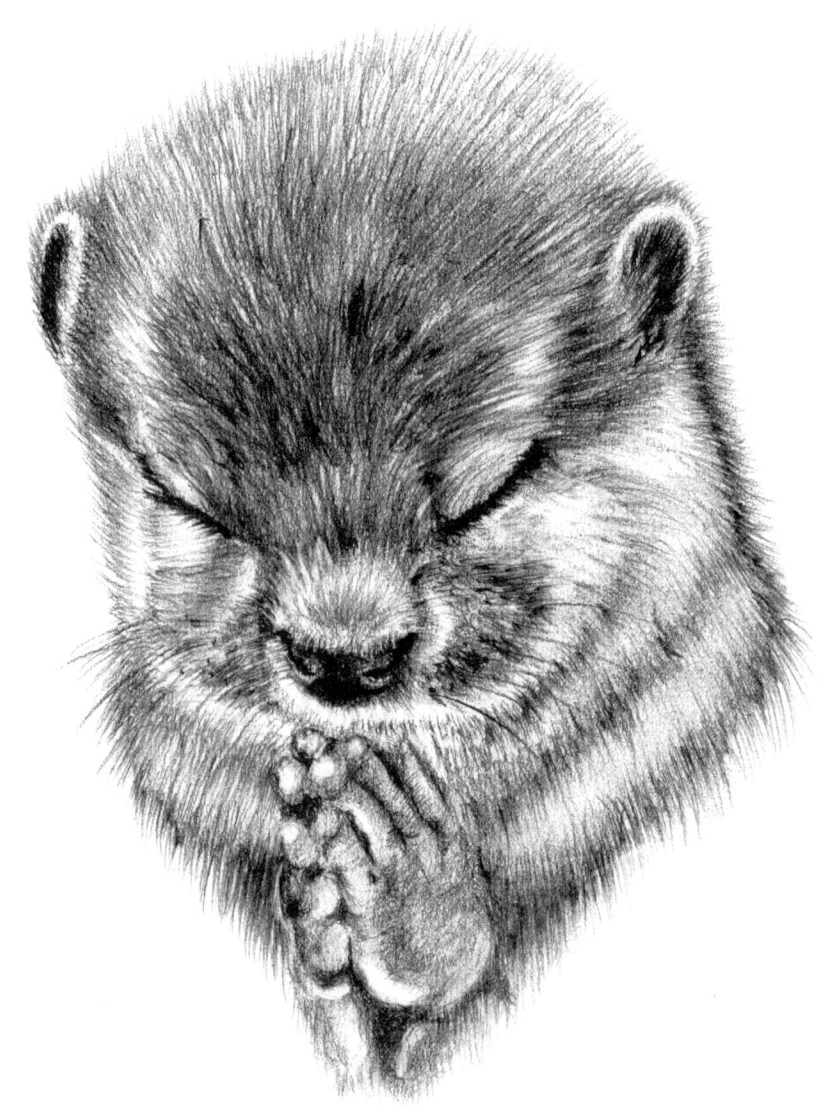

End

"And God saw that it was good. God blessed them and said, 'Be fruitful and increase in number and fill the water in the seas…'" (Genesis 1: 21-22)

"For God so loved the world that He gave His one and only Son, that whoever believes in Him shall not perish but have eternal life.
For God did not send His Son into the world to condemn the world,
but to save the world through Him." (John 3:16-17)

Do you know that God, the powerful Creator of all, loves you and sent His only Son Jesus Christ to this world so you can have eternal life?

I invite you to simply say this prayer:
"Dear Jesus, You have created this amazing world and You have created me.
You love me so that You became a man for me to receive eternal life and to know You.
Jesus I open my heart to You. Please let me know You and come into my life.
In Jesus' Name I pray, Amen."